THE BOOK OF

FINGERPLAYS & ACTION SONGS

Let's Pretend

D1529062

G-5877

THE BOOK OF

FINGERPLAYS & ACTION SONGS

Let's Pretend

Compiled by John M. Feierabend

GIA PUBLICATIONS, INC. · CHICAGO

Compiled by
John M. Feierabend
First Steps in Music, LLC

www.giamusic.com/feierabend

Printed in the
United States of America.
ISBN 1-57999-212-9

Table of
Contents

Introduction

Fingerplays and Action Songs have long been one of the principle joys of childhood. Passed down from generation to generation these songs and rhymes are full of wonder, magic, and makebelieve, making them excellent examples of childhood literature. Furthermore they provide a basis for the musical understandings of form and expression.

Each phrase has a motion; each new phrase - a new motion and the structure of the song or rhyme is assimilated through movement. The expressiveness of the melody or spoken rhyme is reflected in the expressive movement that accompanies. Hence these songs and rhymes introduce the artful expressiveness that can be experienced in more sophisticated classical, folk and jazz musics.

Fingerplays and Action Songs plant the seeds for the wonder, the structure and expressive qualities that can be found in all great music.

Here are some well known and some not so well known songs and rhymes that are delicious as well as good for you!

John M. Feierabend

FINGERPLAYS

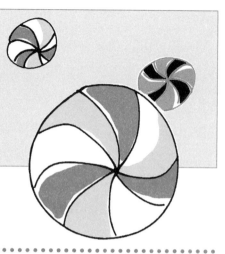

Bouncing Around...

A Ball for Baby

Here's a ball for baby, big and soft and round.
Touch fingertips of one hand to the fingertips of the other.
Here is baby's hammer, see how he can pound!
Tap one fist onto the other fist.
Here are baby's soldiers, standing in a row.
Hold fingers stiff and straight.
This is baby's music, clapping, clapping so!
Clap hands together.
Here is baby's trumpet, tootle-tootle-too.
Hold both hands to mouth as if playing a trumpet.
This is the way baby plays "Peek-a-boo."
Cover eyes and uncover at "Peek-a-boo."
Here's a big umbrella, keeping baby dry.
Push up into the palm of one hand with one finger of the other hand.
Here is baby's cradle, rock-a-baby bye.
Fold arms as if holding a baby and rock back and forth.

I See a Ball

I see a ball,
Touch thumb and index finger of one hand to make a circle.
And I see a ball,
Make a circle with the thumb and index finger of the other hand.
And a great big ball I see.
Make a large circle with both arms.
Help me count them;
One, two, three.
Make each shape again as you count the three balls.

I Can Make a Hammock

I can make a hammock,
Fold hands and open them with palms up.
I can make a cup.
Cup hands together, palms up.
Here's the way to make a ball.
Form a ball with two hands together.
Here's how I toss it up!
Throw "ball" above head and let go of hands.

A Ram Sam Sam *Morocco*

1. A ram, sam, sam, A ram, sam, sam,

2. gu-li, gu-li, gu-li, gu-li, gu-li, ram, sam, sam.

3. A - ra - fi, a - ra - fi,

4. gu-li, gu-li, gu-li, gu-li, gu-li ram, sam, sam.

Motions

During the first phrase pat on legs.

During the second and fourth phrases roll one hand over the other.

During the third phrase spread arms far apart and back twice. Older children can sing this song as a round.

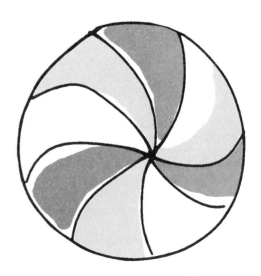

People We Know

Grandma's Glasses

These are grandma's glasses,
*With index finger and thumb of each hand
make circles for each eye to look through.*
And this is grandma's cap,
Place both hands on head.
And this is the way she folds her hands,
Fold hands.
And puts them in her lap.
Set folded hands in lap.

These are grandpa's glasses,
*Make large circles with each hand and
look through.*
And this is grandpa's hat.
Hands and arms straight up and out.
And this is the way he folds his arms,
Fold arms.
Just like that.
*Bounce folded arms up and down three
times.*

Lincoln Hoed

Lincoln hoed the growing corn,
Pretend to hoe the ground.
And chopped the family's wood.
Chop with one hand onto the other.
He built a cabin out of logs,
Pound two fists together.
Read all the books he could.
Hold hands together, palms up.

Mr. Lynn

Mr. Lynn is very thin.
Place palms of hands flat together.
Mr. Pratt is very fat.
Pull hands apart leaving fingertips touching.
Mr. Cort is very short.
Place hands near the floor.
Mr. Hall is very tall.
Place hands above head.
Mr. Dent is very bent.
Make fingers all bent.
But Mr. Wait is very straight.
Make hands straight and stiff.

Miss Polly Had a Dolly

Miss Polly had a dolly who was sick, sick, sick.
Cross arms over stomach and twist side to side.
She phoned for the doctor to come quick, quick, quick.
Hold "phone" to one ear and dial or push buttons with the other hand.
The doctor came with his bag and his hat.
Hold "bag" with one hand and place the other hand on your head.
He knocked on the door with a rat-a-tat-tat.
Knock at an imaginary door.
He looked at the dolly and he shook his head.
Look down and shake head back and forth.
He said, "Miss Polly, put her straight to bed."
Shake one finger.
He wrote on a paper for a pill, pill, pill.
Tap the palm of one hand with a finger of the other hand.
"I'll be back in the morning with the bill, bill, bill."
Wave "good-bye."

Fredrick Fountain

Fred - rick Foun - tain climbed a moun - tain

right up to the ver - y top.

Verse & Motions

Slowly lift hands above head while singing.

Spoken:
He ate his coat and hat and
bag and then poor Fred went POP!
Clap hands together on the word "POP."

John Brown's Baby

John Brown's ba-by had a cold u-pon his chest.

John Brown's ba-by had a cold u-pon his chest.

John Brown's ba-by had a cold u-pon his chest, and he

rubbed it with cam-phor-a-ted oil.

Motions

Leave out a word on each repeated singing and substitute the motion:

baby - *Fold arms and rock "baby" twice.*
cold - *Cough once.*
chest - *Tap chest with one hand.*
rubbed - *Rub chest with one hand.*
camphorated oil - *Hold nose.*

Things That Go

Crocodile Song (She Sailed Away)

She sailed a-way on a bright and sun-ny day, On the back of a croc-o-dile. "You see," said she, "He's as tame as he can be! I'll float him down the Nile!" The croc winked his eye as she waved them all good-bye, Wear-ing a hap-py smile. At the end of the ride the lad-y was in-side, And the smile was on the croc-o-dile!

Motions

She sailed away...
Place one hand flat on the back of the other hand. Rotate thumbs as you "swim" hands back and forth.

"You see," said she...
Shake one finger, then stroke the back of one hand with the other.

The croc winked...
Wink, wave, and then draw a smile in space.

At the end...
Make a sailing motion as in the beginning. At the end of the song clap hands together two times.

El Carro de Mi Jefe (My Boss' Car) *Spanish*

El car-ro de mi je-fe tie-ne hue-co en el cau-cho, El

car-ro de mi je-fe tie-ne hue-co en el cau-cho, El

car-ro de mi je-fe tie-ne hue-co en el cau-cho, Re-pa-

re - mos - lo con chi - cle.

General Translation

The car of my boss has a hole in its tire. Let us fix it with gum.

Motions

carro - *Drive a car.*
jefe - *Tip a hat.*
hueco - *Point a finger and jab as if to puncture.*
caucho - *Draw a circle in the air with same finger.*

Sing the song with all the motions. On each repetition, substitute one more of the words above with "mm." When all of the above words have been substituted, sing the song one more time and substitute "caucho" with a chewing motion. Also try singing with the actions faster and faster.

The Wheels on the Bus

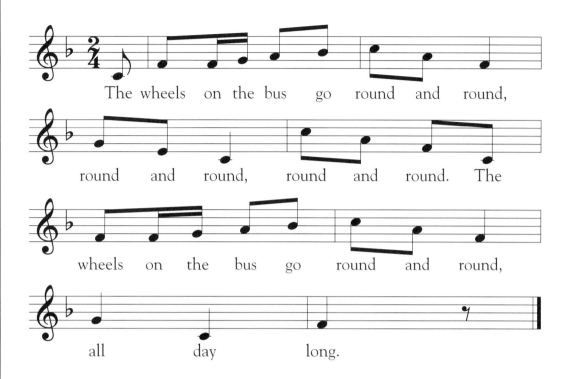

The wheels on the bus go round and round,

round and round, round and round. The

wheels on the bus go round and round,

all day long.

Additional Verses & Motions

1. *During verse 1 roll hands one over the other.*

2. The horn on the bus goes beep, beep, beep... *With open hand, press out front for each "beep."*

3. The wipers on the bus go swish, swish, swish... *With both arms up, palms facing away, sway arms back and forth.*

4. The driver on the bus says, "Move on back,"... *Hold thumb up and gesture over shoulder.*

5. The people on the bus go up and down... *Bounce up and down.*

6. The baby on the bus says, "wah, wah, wah,"... *Rub eyes.*

7. The mother on the bus says, "sh, sh, sh,"... *Make "sh" sounds with one finger placed in front of mouth.*

8. The man on the bus just reads the paper... *Hold up an imaginary paper and turn head from side to side.*

Mother Earth

Green Leaf

Here's a green leaf,
Hold out one hand with palm up.
And here's a green leaf
Hold out other hand, palm up.
That, you see, makes two.
Here is a bud
Cup hands together tightly.
That makes a flower.
Watch it bloom for you!
Slowly unfold hands and extend fingers.

This Is the Sea

This is the sea, the wavy sea.
*Fold arms; alternately lift elbows up and
down.*
Here is a boat,
Cup one hand.
And here is me.
*Place finger of other hand into cupped
hand.*
All the fishes down below,
Wiggle fingers down by the ground.
Wiggle their tails, and away they go.
Put hands behind your back.

Over There the Sun Gets Up

Over there the sun gets up
Extend one arm and point out in front.
And marches all the day.
Raise that arm slowly.
At noon, it stands right overhead;
Point straight up.
At night, it goes away.
Slowly lower arm.

Ahí Esta la Luna (There Is the Moon)   *Spanish*

Ahí esta la luna.
Point to the moon.
Comiendo su tuna.
Bring fingers toward mouth.
Tirando las cascaras
Toss hands out in front.
En la laguna.
Draw a circle in front with one hand.

General Translation

There is the moon
Eating a prickly pear.
Throwing the peelings
In the lake.

Under the Spreading Chestnut Tree

Un - der the spread - ing chest - nut tree,

When I held you on my knee,

We were hap - py as can be,

Un - der the spread - ing chest - nut tree.

Motions

Leave out a word on each repeated singing and substitute the motion.

spreading - *Stretch arms out to the sides.*
chest - *Touch both hands to chest.*
nut - *Touch head.*
tree - *Reach hands above head.*
you - *Point to someone.*
me - *Point to yourself.*
happy - *Push up the corners of mouth with index finger from each hand.*

Pickin' a Spot

Pick - in'   a   spot,   Cut - tin' the weeds down,

Mov - in'   the   rocks,   Clear - in'   the   land.

Dig - gin'   a   hole,   Put - tin'   the   seeds   in,

Pat - tin'   it   down,   Watch - in'   it   grow.

Rain   falls,   Sun   shines,

Trees   grow.   Ap - ples!   Whoa!

Motions by Measure

1 - Shade eyes with hand and look back and forth.
2 - Make chopping motions with hands.
3 - Lift and move pretend rocks.
4 - Spread hands apart.
5 - Pretend to dig.
6 - Pretend to plant seeds in the palm of one hand.
7 - Pat seeds in palm.
8 - Touch fingertips to thumb to make a hole. Other hand "grows" up through the hole.
9 - Make rain motion with fingers.
10 - Hold hands above head with hands touching each other.
11 - Bring fists up slowly.
12 - Hands burst open.

This Is the Tree

This is the tree with leaves so green,
Hold up arms with fingers spread apart.
Here are the apples that hang in between,
Make two fists and hold in front.
When the wind blows the apples will fall,
Lower fists to the ground.
Here is the basket to gather them all.
Hold hands together, palms up.

Up the Apple Tree

I climbed up the apple tree,
Pantomime climbing motion.
All the apples fell on me!
Tap hands on head one after the other.
Apple pudding, apple pie,
Tap both legs, cross hands and tap, uncross and tap, cross and tap.
Did you ever tell a lie?
Shake finger.
Maybe yes, maybe no.
Place one hand out to side with palm up, place the other hand to the side with palm up.
Maybe yes, well... I don't know!
Place the first hand out to side with palm up and then shrug shoulders.

Kahuli Aku (Little Tree Shell) *Hawaiian*

Ka - hu - li a - ku, Ka - hu - li mai;

Ka - hu - li lei 'u - la lei 'a - ko - le - a.

Ko - le - a, ko - le - a, ki - 'i i ka wai

wai 'a - ko - le - a, wai 'a - ko - lea, Ah,——

Ah.——

General Translation

Turn little tree shell, turn back
  again.
Here is a red lei, a lei of ferns.
Little bird, fetch nectar from the
  akolea flower.

Kahuli is the Hawaiian tree shell *Pupu
  Kani Oe.*

*'Akolea is a native fern with large beau-
  tiful, lacy fronds.*

*Kolea is a migrating bird that comes to
  Hawaii in the end of August and
  leaves in May for Siberia or Alaska.*

Motions

Kahuli aku - *Right hand crosses in front while hand turns back and forth.*

Kahuli mai - *Left hand crosses in front while hand turns back and forth.*

Kahuli lei 'ula - *Turn both hands back and forth and place lei over shoulders.*

Lei 'akolea - *Both hands "pick a flower" and reach in front with the flower.*

Kolea, kolea - *Reach arms out to side and slowly flap two times.*

Ki'i i ka wai - *Dive and dip both hands in front.*

Wai 'akolea - *Dip hands once and show flower in front.*

Wai 'akolea - *Dip hands once and show flower in front.*

The last two measures represent the sound of the tree shell.

Hands & Shoulders, Knees & Thumbs

Tommy Thumb

Tommy Thumb up.
Hold thumbs up.
Tommy Thumb down.
Point thumbs down.
Tommy Thumb dancing all around
the town.
Make circles in the air with thumbs.

Repeat with:
Peter Pointer
Toby Tall Man
Ruby Finger
Baby Finger
Finger Family

Oh, Chester, Have You Heard?

Oh, Chester - *Touch chest.*
Have you heard - *Touch ear.*
About Harry? - *Touch hair.*
He just got back - *Touch back.*
From the army. - *Touch arm.*
I hear - *Touch ear.*
He knows - *Touch nose.*
How to wear a rose. - *Draw circle on chest.*
Hip, Hip - *With both hands tap on hips twice.*
Hooray - *Raise arms.*
For the army. - *Touch arm.*
Oh, - *Touch thumb to forefinger.*
I - *Touch near eye.*
Say, - *Touch mouth.*
Have you heard - *Touch ear.*
About Harry? - *Touch hair.*
He just - *Touch chest.*
Got back - *Touch back.*
From the next - *Touch neck.*
To the front - *Touch chest.*
Where he's needed - *Touch knee.*
At the foot - *Touch foot.*
Of the army. - *Touch arm.*
Everybody - *Spread arms wide.*
Knows - *Touch nose.*
About Harry. - *Touch hair.*
Hip, Hip - *With both hands tap on hips twice.*
Hooray - *Raise arms.*
For the army. - *Touch arm.*

Open, Shut Them

O - pen, shut them, o - pen shut them, Give a lit - tle clap.

O - pen, shut them, o - pen shut them, Lay them in your lap.

Motions

Open and shut hands and perform motions as indicated.

Verse 2

Creep them, creep them, gently creep them
Right up to your chin.
Open wide your little mouth
But do not let them in!

Motions

Continue to perform motions as indicated, then quickly hide hands behind back at the end.

Do Your Ears Hang Low?

Do your ears hang low? Do they wob-ble to and

fro? Can you tie them in a knot? Can you

tie them in a bow? Can you throw them o-ver your

should-er, like a con-tin-en-tal sold-ier? Do your

ears hang low?

Verse & Motions

Do your ears hang low?
Wave hands with thumbs touching near ears.
Do they wobble to and fro?
Place palms together and push back and forth.
Can you tie them in a knot?
Roll hands one over the other.
Can you tie them in a bow?
Pull hands apart.

Can you throw them over your shoulder,
Hold hands together and lift up to one shoulder.
Like a Continental soldier?
Salute with one hand.
Do your ears hang low?
With thumbs touching near ears, wave hands.

Sing each repeat a little faster.

How Many? So Many!

Two Little Apples

Two little apples,
  Make two fists.
Hanging in a tree.
  Point up.
Two little apples,
  Make two fists again.
Smiled at me.
  Touch mouth and smile.
I shook that tree as hard as I could,
  *With both hands hold the imaginary tree
  and shake.*
Down came the apples,
Ummmm, they were good.
  Rub tummy.

Two Tall Telephone Poles

Two tall telephone poles,
  Hold up the index finger of both hands.
Between them a wire is strung.
  *With index fingers still up, touch middle
  fingers of each hand together.*
Two little birds hopped onto the wire,
  *Touch thumbs of both hands to the middle
  fingers.*
And they swung, swung, swung.
  *Still holding hands together, swing hands
  back and forth.*

Two Little Houses

Two little houses closed up tight
  Make two tight fists touching.
Let's open the windows and let in
  some light.
  *Lift the index finger of each hand making a
  window.*
Ten little finger people tall and
  straight,
  Hold fingers out straight.
Ready for the bus at half-past eight.
  Fingers wiggle and hide behind back.

Two Old Gentlemen

Two old gentlemen,
  Hold two thumbs up.
Met in a glen,
Bowed most politely,
  Bend one thumb.
Bowed one again.
  Bend the other thumb.
How do you do?
  Bend one thumb.
How do you do?
  Bend the other thumb.
And how do you do again?
  Bend both thumbs.

  Repeat with each finger.
2. Two thin ladies...
3. Two tall policemen...
4. Two happy school children...
5. Two little babies...

Mein Hut (My Hat It Has Three Corners) *German*

Mein Hut, der hat drei Ec - ken,
Drei

My hat it has three cor - ners,
Three

eck - en hat mein Hut.
Und

cor - ners has my hat.
And

hätt' er nicht drei eck - en,
It

had it not three cor - ners,
It

Es wäre nicht mein Hut.

would not be my hat.

Motions

*Leave out another word on each repeated
singing and substitute the motion.*

My - *Point to self.*
hat - *Point to head.*
three - *Hold up three fingers.*
corners - *Point to elbow.*

This Old Man

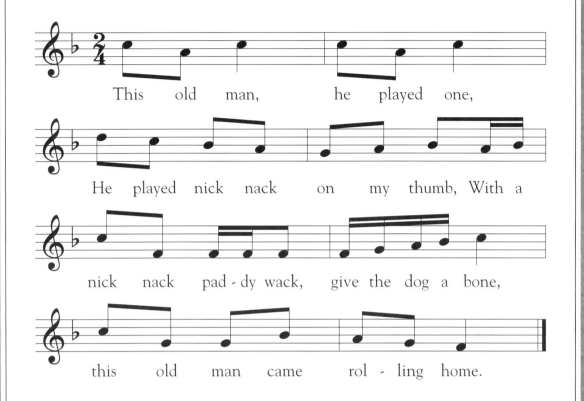

This old man, he played one,

He played nick nack on my thumb, With a

nick nack pad-dy wack, give the dog a bone,

this old man came rol-ling home.

Verse

2. ... two... on my shoe...
3. ... three... on my knee...
4. ... four... on the floor...
5. ... five... making a dive...
6. ... six... with some sticks...
7. ... seven... up in heaven...
8. ... eight... on my gate...
9. ... nine... on my spine...
10. ... ten... once again...

Motions

knick knack
  Pat knees two times.
paddy whack
  Clap hands two times.
give the dog a bone
  Place one hand out in front, palm up.
this old man came rolling home
  Roll hands one over the other.

Five Little Ladies

Five little ladies going for a walk,
Begin with both hands behind your back;
bring one hand out tapping on the floor.
Five little ladies stopping for a talk.
Tap the tips of your fingers together.
Along came five little gentlemen,
Bring other hand out from behind back
while tapping on the floor.
They all danced together and then
there were ten.
Fold hands and sway them back and forth.

Five Little Leaves

Five little leaves so bright and gay,
Hold up one hand and wave it back and
forth.
Were dancing about the tree one day.
The wind came blowing through the
town,
Blow on the hand.
One little leaf came tumbling down.
Hold up one finger, and wave it back and
forth while lowering hand to the floor.

Repeat with "Four little leaves" until there
are no leaves left.

Five Little Peas

Five little peas in a pea pod pressed,
Make a fist.
One grew,
Show one finger.
Two grew,
Show two fingers.
And so did the rest.
Show all five fingers.
They grew and grew and did not stop,
Until one day they all went POP!
Gradually spread hands further apart from
each other and clap hands with the last
word.

Five Little Jack-o'-Lanterns

Five little jack-o'-lanterns sitting on a
gate,
The first one said, "It's getting late."
The second one said, "I heard a
noise."
The third one said, "It's just some
boys."
The fourth one said, "Let's run, let's
run."
The fifth one said, "Let's stay and
have fun."
When "OOOH," went the wind and
blew out the light,
And away they ran on Halloween
night.

Five Little Pumpkins

Five little pumpkins sitting on a gate,
Rest five fingers of one hand on the other arm.

The first one said, "Oh my, it's getting late."
Hold the thumb of one hand with the other hand and then place both hands on cheeks.

The second one said, "There are witches in the air."
Hold the index finger of one hand with the other hand and then make a circle motion above your head.

The third one said, "But we don't care."
Hold the middle finger of one hand with the other hand and then hold hands out and shake head "no."

The fourth one said, "Let's run, run, run."
Hold the fourth finger of one hand with the other hand and then quickly alternate hands patting on legs.

The fifth one said, "I'm ready for fun."
Hold the little finger of one hand with the other hand and then with palms together quickly slide them back and forth.

"Ooooooh" went the wind,
Shake hands around.

And out went the light,
Clap hands once.

And the five little pumpkins
Rolled out of sight.
Roll hands one over the other and then put them behind your back.

I Love Sixpence

I love six-pence, jol-ly lit-tle six-pence.

I love six-pence bet-ter than my life.

I spent a pen-ny of it, I lent a pen-ny of it,

And I took four-pence home to my wife.

Verse 2

I love fourpence, jolly little
  fourpence,
I love fourpence better than my
  life.
I spent a penny of it, I lent a
  penny of it,
And I took twopence home to
  my wife.

Verse 3

I love twopence, jolly little
  twopence,
I love twopence better than my
  life.
I spent a penny of it, I lent a
  penny of it,
And I took nothing home to my
  wife.

Verse 4

I love nothing, jolly little nothing,
What will nothing buy for my
  wife?
I spent nothing, I lent nothing,
I love nothing better than my
  wife.

*Hold up six fingers and sway back and
forth. As you "spend" each penny put that
finger down. At the end hold both hands
out, palms up, and shake head.*

Ten Little Candles

Ten little candles on a chocolate cake.
Hold up ten fingers.
"Whoo, whoo," and then there were eight.
Blow on the thumb of each hand and fold thumbs under.
Eight little candles on candlesticks,
Hold up four fingers on each hand.
"Whoo, whoo," and then there were six.
Blow on the next finger on each hand and fold under.
Six little candles and not one more,
Hold up three fingers on each hand.
"Whoo, whoo," and then there were four.
Blow on the next finger on each hand and fold under.
Four little candles, red, white and blue,
Hold up two fingers on each hand.
"Whoo, whoo," and then there were two.
Blow on the next finger on each hand and fold under.
Two little candles standing in the sun,
Hold up one finger on each hand.
"Whoo, whoo," and now there are none.
Blow on the last finger on each hand and fold under.

Ten Little Soldiers

Ten little soldiers stand up straight,
Hold hands up with fingers very straight.
Ten little soldiers make a gate.
Fold hands and flatten hands to make a wall.
Ten little soldiers make a ring,
Form a circle with both hands.
Ten little soldiers bow to the king.
Bend fingers on both hands.
Ten little soldiers dance all day,
Wiggle fingers.
Ten little soldiers hide away.
Quickly place hands behind back.

How Many Animals? So Many Animals!

Two Little Blackbirds

Two little blackbirds
Sitting on a hill.
*Sit holding both thumbs up while bouncing
fists on knees.*
One named Jack,
Raise one thumb up.
And one named Jill.
Raise the other thumb up.
Fly away Jack,
Place one hand behind your back.
Fly away Jill.
Place the other hand behind your back.
Come back Jack,
Bring one thumb back out.
Come back Jill.
Bring the other thumb back out.

Variation

Two little chicky birds sittin' on a
wall,
One named Peter and one named
Paul.
Fly away Peter. Fly away Paul.
Come back Peter. Come back Paul.
Two little chicky birds sittin' on a
wall.

Five Little Fishes Swimming

Five little fishes were swimming near
the shore,
One took a dive and then there were
four.
*"Swim" one hand up and down and at the
end fold under the thumb.*
Four little fishes were swimming out
to sea,
One went for food and then there
were three.
*"Swim" hand up and down and fold
another finger under.*
Three little fishes said, "Now, what
shall we do?"
One swam away and then there were
two.
*"Swim" hand up and down and fold
another finger under.*
Two little fishes were having great fun,
But one took a plunge and then there
was one.
*"Swim" hand up and down and fold
another finger under.*
One little fish says, "I like the warm
sun,"
Away he went and then there were
none.
"Swim" the last finger behind your back.

Three Little Ducks

Three little ducks went out to play
Hold up three fingers.
Over the hill and far away.
Raise the three fingers and place them behind your back.
Mother Duck called, "Quack, quack, quack."
With the other hand touch fingers to thumb three times.
Two little ducks came waddling back.
Bring two fingers from behind your back.

Two little ducks went out to play
Hold up two fingers.
Over the hill and far away.
Raise the two fingers and place them behind your back.
Mother Duck called, "Quack, quack, quack."
With the other hand touch fingers to thumb three times.
One little duck came waddling back.
Bring one finger from behind your back.

One little duck went out to play
Hold up index finger.
Over the hill and far away.
Raise index finger and place it behind your back.
Mother Duck called, "Quack, quack, quack."
With the other hand touch fingers to thumb three times.
No little ducks came waddling back.
Hold hands out to sides with palms up and shake head "no."

"Please, please, please come back."
Place hands behind back.
Three little ducks came waddling back.
Bring three fingers from behind your back.

Three Little Squirrels

There were three little squirrels
  Hold up three fingers.
Sittin' in the shade.
  *Cup other hand and hold it over the three
  fingers.*
Said one little squirrel, "I'm not
  afraid."
  *Cross arms across chest and swing from
  side to side.*
Along came the hunter
  Point thumb and index finger of each hand.
And Boom!
  Clap hands.
Did those little squirrels run!
  Quickly place hands behind back.

Ten Little Squirrels

Ten little squirrels up in a tree.
  Ten fingers outspread.
The first two said, "What?"
  Hold up thumbs.
The next two said, "A man with a
gun."
  Hold up pointer fingers.
The next two said, "Let's run, let's
run."
  Hold up middle fingers.
The next two said, "Let's hide in the
shade."
  Hold up ring fingers.
The last two said, "We're not afraid."
  Hold up little fingers.
Bang! went the gun.
  Clap hands.
Away they all ran.
  Scamper fingers away behind your back.

Five Crayfish

Five crayfish sat on the sandy seabed
Start with both hands behind your back.

Waving their feelers in front of their heads.
Bring one hand out and wave five fingers back and forth in front.

Out of a cave came a long moray eel
Bring out the other hand waving it back and forth.

And he gobbled one up for his midday meal.
Clap hands on "gobbled" and return hands behind your back. Repeat until no crayfish are left.

Two Mother Pigs

Two mother pigs lived in a pen,
Hold up both thumbs.

Each had four babies and that made ten.
Hold up ten fingers.

These four babies were black as night.
Show four fingers of one hand.

These four babies were black and white.
Show four fingers of the other hand.

But all eight babies loved to play,
Show four fingers of both hands.

And they rolled and they rolled in the mud all day.
Roll hands over each other.

Three Little Monkeys

Three little monkeys jumping on the bed,
Tap three fingers of one hand onto the palm of the other hand.

One fell out and bumped his head.
Show one finger and then hold head with both hands.

Mama called the doctor and the doctor said,
Hold "phone" to ear with one hand and dial or push buttons with the other hand.

"No more monkeys jumping on the bed."
Shake one finger as if scolding. Repeat until no monkeys are left.

Variation

Two little monkeys
Fighting in bed.
Tap two fingers from one hand onto the palm of the other hand.

One fell out
Show one finger.

And hurt his head
Hold head and shake it back and forth.

The other called the doctor
Pretend to call on the phone.

And the doctor said,
"That's what you get for fighting in bed."
Shake one finger at "monkeys."

See, See, See, Three Birds Are in a Tree

See, see, see, three birds are in a tree.

One can chirp and one can sing, One is just a ti-ny thing.

See, see, see, three birds are in a tree.

Additional Verse & Motions

See, see, see,
  Shade eyes.
Three birds are in a tree.
  Hold up three fingers.
One can chirp and one can sing,
  *With one finger, point to the first and
  second finger of the other hand.*
One is just a tiny thing;
  Cup hands.
See, see, see,
  Shade eyes.
Three birds are in a tree.
  Hold up three fingers.

Look, look, look,
  Shade eyes.
Three ducks are in a brook.
  Hold up three fingers.
One is white and one is brown,
  *With one finger, point to the first and
  second finger of the other hand.*
One is swimming upside down;
  Bend over and touch head to floor.
Look, look, look,
  Shade eyes.
Three ducks are in a brook.
  Hold up three fingers.

Five Little Mice Came Out to Play

Five little mice came out to play,
Gathering crumbs along the way;
Begin with both hands behind your back and slowly bring one hand out tapping on the floor.

Out came the pussycat, sleek and fat,
Bring other hand out tapping on the floor and "pounce" on the first hand.

Four little mice went scampering back.
Return both hands behind your back while tapping on the floor. Repeat until "No little mice went scampering back."

On the Pantry Floor

Five little mice on the pantry floor,
Tap all five fingers of one hand on the floor.

This little mouse peeked behind the door.
With one finger tap on the thumb of the other hand and fold the thumb under.

This little mouse nibbled at the cake.
Tap on the next finger and fold under.

This little mouse not a sound did make.
Tap on the next finger and fold under.

This little mouse took a bit of cheese.
Tap on the next finger and fold under.

This little mouse heard the kitten sneeze.
Tap on last finger and fold under.

"Ah-choo," sneezed the kitten, and "squeak" they all cried,
Quickly open both hands with the sneeze and raise hands in fright.

As they found a hole and ran inside.
Fold arms and place hands in opposite armpits.

More Animal Friends

The Monkeys and the Crocodile

Five little monkeys swinging in a tree
   Swing hand to and fro with a limp wrist.
Teasing Mr. Crocodile, "You can't catch me."
   Hold thumbs by ears and wiggle fingers.
Along came Mr. Crocodile, quiet as can be....
SNAP!
   Clap hands (Crocodile eats one monkey).

Continue until only one monkey is left. At the last line the monkey jumps away and is not caught and says, "Ha, ha, you missed me!" and again hold thumbs by ears and wiggle fingers.

A Slippery Snake

I saw a slippery, slithering snake
   Place palms together and wave hands side to side.
Slide through the grasses, making them shake.

He looked at me with his beady eye,
   Look through hands shaped like glasses.
"Go away from my pretty green garden," said I,
   Point away.
"Ssss," said the slippery, slithering snake
As he slid through the grasses, making them shake.
   Place palms together, waving hands from side to side.

I Had a Little Pig

I had a little pig and I fed him in a trough,
   Pat the beat on legs.
He got so fat that his tail popped off!
   Spread hands wider and wider apart.
I got me a hammer,
   Make a fist with one hand.
I got me a nail
   Make a fist with the other hand.
And I made that pig a homemade tail!
   Pound fists together on the beat.

Eensy Weensy Spider

Een - sy ween - sy spi - der went up the wa - ter spout.

Down came the rain and washed the spi - der out.

Out came the sun and dried up all the rain, And the

een - sy ween - sy spi - der went up the spout a - gain.

Line 1

Touching fingertips of one hand to the other hand, wiggle fingers while moving low to high above head.

Line 2

With hands apart, wiggle fingers and lower hands. Cross hands in front and quickly spread them apart.

Line 3

Touch hands together above head and slowly separate and lower them.

Line 4

Move hands as in line 1.

Alle Meine Entchen (All My Little Ducklings) *German*

Al - le mei - ne   Ent - chen,   schwim - men   auf   dem

See,   schwim - men   auf   dem   See.

Köpf - chen in das Was - ser, Schwänz-chen in die   Höh'.

Köpf - chen in das Was - ser, Schwänz - en in die Höh'.

General Translation

All my little ducklings are
   swimming in the lake.
Little heads in the water,
Little tails in the air.

Motions

*While sitting, move both hands as if
   swimming.*
Touch head to floor.
With both hands pretend to wiggle tail.

There Was a Little Turtle

There was a little turtle
Make a fist with one hand.
Who lived in a box.
Cover the fist with the other hand.
He swam in the water,
Swimming motion alternating hands.
He climbed on the rocks.
Make a fist with one hand and walk across the knuckles with the fingers of the other hand.
He snapped at a minnow,
On the word "snapped" reach out and quickly put all fingertips together.
He snapped at a flea,
He snapped at a mosquito
And he snapped at me!
He caught the minnow.
On the word "caught" clap hands once.
He caught the flea.
He caught the mosquito
But he didn't catch me!
Point to yourself and shake head "no."

This Is My Turtle

This is my turtle,
Make a fist with the thumb extended.
He lives in a shell.
Fold thumb under.
He likes his home very well.
Nod head "yes".
He pokes his head out,
Pop thumb back out.
When he wants to eat.
And pulls it back
Fold thumb under again.
When he wants to sleep.
Place palms together and rest head on hands.

Fishy, Fishy in a Brook

Fishy, fishy in a brook.
Place palms together and wiggle hands.
Papa caught him with a hook.
Pretend to cast out a fishing line.
Mama fried him in a pan.
With both hands pretend to hold the handle of a frying pan and shake the pan.
Baby ate him like a man.
Pretend to nibble on the fish.

Here Is a Frog

Here is a frog
Make a fist with one hand.
And here is a pond.
Open palm of other hand.
A frog in a pond am I.
Set fist on open palm.
I can jump so far,
Throw fist out sideways.
I can jump so high,
Throw fist upward.
Hippity, hippity, hop.
Bounce fist in palm three times.
I sit on a lily pad high and dry
Place fist on the back of other hand.
And watch the fishes swimming by,
Wiggle fingers of both hands while moving fingers back and forth.
Then splash!
Clap hands once.
How I make the water fly,
Throw hands up and apart.
Hippity, hippity, hop.
Bounce fist in palm three times.

Furry Friends

Bunny with Ears So Funny

Here's a bunny with ears so funny
Hold up one fist with two fingers raised.
And here is his hole in the ground.
Touch thumb to tips of fingers on other hand.
At the first sound he hears, he wig -
gles his ears
And jumps right into the ground.
*Place the two upheld fingers of one hand
into the "hole" made by the other hand.*

A Great Big Cat

A great big cat
Hold hands far apart.
And a wee little mouse,
Hold hands close together.
Ran round and round
Roll hands, one over the other.
In a high, high house.
*Hold arms above head with fingertips
touching.*
But the wee little mouse
Hold hands close together.
Got caught at last,
Clap hands on "caught."
'Cause the great big cat
Hold hands far apart.
Ran round so fast.
*Roll hands, one over the other faster and
faster.*

Whisky, Frisky

Whisky, frisky, hippity-hop,
Wiggle fingers of one hand on the floor.
Up he goes to the treetop.
*Wiggle fingers from floor, up body and up
one upraised arm.*
Whirly, twirly, round and round,
Roll one hand over the other.
Down he scampers to the ground.
*Wiggle fingers of one hand down upraised
arm to the floor.*
Furly, curly, what a tail,
*Move one hand in circular motions from
the wrist.*
Tall as a feather, broad as a snail!
Reach one hand up high and spread fingers.
Where is his supper? In the shell.
Cup hands together.
Snappety, crackity, out it fell.
Pull hands apart pretending to drop the nut.

Gray Squirrel

Gray squir-rel, gray squir-rel, swish your bush-y tail.

Gray squir-rel, gray squir-rel, swish your bush-y tail.

Wrin-kle up your fun-ny nose. Hold a nut be-tween your toes.

Gray squir-rel, gray squir-rel, swish your bush-y tail.

Motions

Lines 1 & 2

Hold hands together in front of body and sway back and forth.

Line 3

Wrinkle nose repeatedly; hold hands in a ball.

Line 4

Hold hands together in front of body and sway back and forth.

Birdie, Birdie

Here's a Nest

Here's a nest for robin,
Cup hands together.
Here's a hive for bee.
Touch fingertips of one hand to the other.
Here's a hole for rabbit,
Make a big circle with both arms.
And here's a house for me.
Touch hands together with arms held above your head.

Here Is the Ostrich

Here is the ostrich straight and tall,
Raise one arm with hand drooping over.
Nodding his head above us all.
Raise and lower hand from wrist.
Here is the long snake on the ground,
Move hand back and forth in a wavy motion.
Wriggling upon the stones he found.
Here are the birds that fly so high,
Flap arms.
Spreading their wings across the sky.

Here is the hedgehog, prickly and small,
Make a fist.
Rolling himself into a ball.
Here is the spider scuttling around,
Wiggle fingertips of one hand around on the floor.
Treading so lightly on the ground.
Here are the children fast asleep,
Rest head on hands held together.
And here at night the owls do peep.
With thumbs and forefingers make "glasses" to look through.

A Big-Eyed Owl

There's a big-eyed owl
With fingers draw circles around eyes.
With a pointed nose.
Slide fingers down nose to tip of nose.
With two pointed ears
Hold up index finger of each hand and place hands with fingers extending from head.
And claws for his toes.
Curve fingers and reach hands out in front.
He lives high in a tree
Point up into the air.
And when he looks at you
Point to child.
He flaps his wings
Bend arms at elbows and flap.
And says, "Woo, Woo, Woo."
Make hands like a megaphone.

Mr. Turkey Took a Walk

Mr. Turkey took a walk one day
In the very best of weather.
*Spread fingers of one hand apart and wave
hand back and forth.*
Along came Mr. Duck
And they both talked together.
*Spread fingers of the other hand and bring
toward other hand while waving.*
"Gobble, gobble, gobble."
Open and close "turkey" hand.
"Quack, quack, quack."
Open and close "duck" hand.
"Good-bye." "Good-bye."
Open and close one hand, then the other.
And they both walked back.
Place both hands behind your back.

A Sparrow's Home

A sparrow's home is a nest in the tree.
*Cup one hand, palm up. Place the finger-
tips of the other hand in the cupped palm.*
An octopus's house is a cave beneath
the sea.
Hook thumbs together and wiggle fingers.
In a hole in the ground a little rabbit
hides,
*Close fingers around thumb; slowly lift
thumb, straighten, bend a little.*
A sunflower is where a little gnome
resides.
*Hold palm flat, spread fingers, and rest
other hand in the palm.*
A hollowed-out log is for the porcu-
pine,
*Place cupped hand palm down on the table
or lap. Move the other hand inside.*
But the best home of all is the one
that's mine.
*Touching fingertips together, hold hands
above head.*

Birdie,
Birdie

Squeek, Squeek!

Where Are the Baby Mice?

Where are the baby mice? Squeak, squeak, squeak.
Place one fist in the opposite armpit.
I cannot see them. Peek, peek, peek.
Shade eyes with the other hand and look from side to side.
Here they come from the hole in the wall,
Slowly remove fist from armpit.
One, two, three, four, five; that's all!
Open fingers one at a time.

Little Mousie Brown

Up the tall white candlestick
Raise one arm up.
Crept little Mousie Brown;
Walk up arm with two fingers of the other hand.
Right to the top but he couldn't get down.
Hold onto the fingertips of the up-stretched hand.
So he called to his Grandma,
Cup hands to mouth.
"Grandma, Grandma,"
But grandma was in town.
So he curled himself into a ball
Make fists with both hands.
And rolled himself down.
Starting high and ending low, roll one hand over the other.

The Little Mice Go Creeping

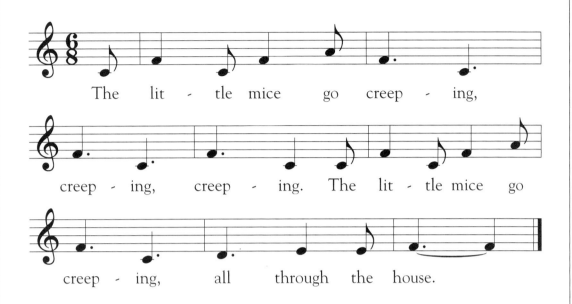

The lit - tle mice go creep - ing,

creep - ing, creep - ing. The lit - tle mice go

creep - ing, all through the house.

Verse 1

Put both hands behind your back.
Bring out one hand with fingers gently
walking.

Verse 2

The big grey cat goes stalking,
stalking, stalking.
The big grey cat goes stalking, all
through the house.
Bring other hand out in larger walking
motions.

Verse 3

The little mice go scampering,
scampering, scampering.
The little mice go scampering, all
through the house.
Wiggle fingers quickly, moving hand
around until hidden behind your back.

Buggie Friends

A Caterpillar Crawled

A caterpillar crawled to the top of a tree.
With two fingers of one hand, climb up the other arm.
"I think I'll take a nap."
So, under a leaf he began to creep
With two fingers walk into the palm of the other hand.
To spin a cocoon;
Rub one hand on the back of the other hand.
Then he fell asleep.
Rest head on two hands with palms together.
All winter he slept in his cocoon bed,
Place one hand on top of the back of the other fist.
'Til spring came along one day and said,
"Wake up, wake up, little sleepyhead.
Shake one hand with the other hand.
Wake up, it's time to get out of bed."
So he opened his eyes that sunshiny day,
Spread fingers wide apart.
Lo! He was a butterfly, and flew away!
Flutter hands away behind your back.

Here Is the Beehive

Here is the beehive, where are the bees?
Make a fist with thumb enclosed.
Hidden away where nobody sees.
Place other hand over the "Hive."
Watch and you'll see them come out of the hive.
Look closely at your hands.
One, two, three, four, five.
Slowly, beginning with the thumb, open each finger.
Bzzzzzzzzzzz.
Flutter fingers away and hide them behind your back.

Sleepy Caterpillars

"Let's go to sleep," the little caterpillars said,
Place fingers of one hand onto the palm of the other hand.
As they tucked themselves into their beds.
Fold open hand around fingers of other hand.
They will awaken by and by,
Slowly open hand.
And each one will be a lovely butterfly.
Flutter both hands up into the air.

Fuzzy Wuzzy Caterpillar

Fuzzy wuzzy caterpillar,
  *Creep fingers of one hand up the other
  arm.*
Into a corner will creep.
He'll spin himself a blanket,
  Roll hands one over the other.
And then fall fast asleep.
  *Place palms together and rest head on
  hands.*
Fuzzy wuzzy caterpillar,
  Lift head, open eyes and stretch.
Wakes up by and by.
Stretches his lovely wings,
Then away the moth will fly!
  *Hook thumbs together and flutter hands
  around.*

Yummy in My Tummy

Here's a Cup

Here's a cup and here's a cup,
Make a circle with one thumb and forefinger; twice.
And here's a pot of tea.
Make a fist with the other hand.
Pour a cup, pour a cup,
With the fisted hand, extend thumb and "pour" into "cup."
And have a drink with me.
Pretend to drink.

Here Is a Saucer

Here is a saucer,
Hold open the palm of one hand.
Here is the cup.
Set the fist of the other hand in the open palm.
Pour in the milk,
Remove open palm hand and pour into the fist.
And drink it up.
Lift fist to mouth.

Zucker und Kaffee German (Sugar and Coffee)

„Grüß Gott, Grüß Gott, was wollen sie?"
„Zucker und Kaffee."
„Da herben Sie's, da haben Sie's"
„Ade, ade, ade."

General Translation

"Hello, hello, what do you want?"
"Sugar and coffee"
"Here you are. Here you are."
"Bye, bye, bye."

With hands straight, touch fingertips together to form roof. Fold down index fingers, one on top of the other to form a counter. Bring little fingers forward through the arch made by the fingers. Wiggle the little fingers when the shopkeeper speaks and wiggle the thumbs when the customer speaks.

Chop, Chop, Chippity Chop

Chop, chop, chippity chop,
With the side of one hand tap on the other arm.
Cut off the bottom and cut off the top
Continue tapping.
What there is left,
Scoop up pile of chopped vegetables.
We'll put in the pot.
Place vegetables in pot.
Chop, chop, chippity chop.
Resume tapping on arm.

Pop, Pop, Pop!

Pop, pop, pop!
Clap hands three times.
Pour the popcorn in the pot.
Pretend to pour into a pot.
Pop, pop, pop!
Clap hands three times.
Take and shake it 'till it's hot.
Hold hands together and shake.
Pop, pop, pop!
Clap hands three times.
Lift the lid. What have you got?
Pretend to lift lid.
Pop, pop, pop, pop, POPCORN!
Clap hands five times and with the last clap spread arms far apart.

Mix a Pancake

Mix a pancake,
Pretend to mix batter in a bowl.
Stir a pancake,
Pop it in a pan.
Pretend to pour batter into a frying pan.
Fry a pancake,
Shake the pan back and forth.
Toss a pancake,
Lift the pan up.
Catch it if you can!
Pretend to catch the pancake.

Peanut on a Railroad Track

A peanut sat on a railroad track,
Cup hands as if holding a peanut.
His heart was all a flutter.
Tap with hand on chest over heart.
Along came the five-fifteen,
Chugging motions with arms.
Uh-oh, peanut butter!
Hold the sides of face with hands.

A Pumpkin for Pie

Here's a pumpkin for the pie.
Make a large circle with arms out in front.
Apples red to bake.
Hold up two fists.
Turkey for the roasting pan,
Hold up fists with thumbs extended.
I can hardly wait!
Rub palms together quickly.

These Are Mother's Knives and Forks

These   are   moth - er's   knives   and   forks.   And

this   is   fa - ther's   ta   -   ble.

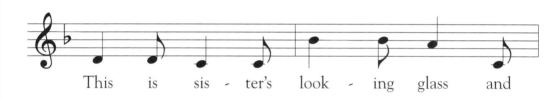

This   is   sis - ter's   look - ing   glass   and

this   is   the   ba - by's   cra   -   dle.

Motions

These are mother's knives and forks
Hold both hands back to back with fingers intertwined.

And this is father's table.
Roll hands over to show the knuckles.

This is sister's looking glass,
Raise and touch each index finger to each other.

And this is the baby's cradle.
Raise and touch each baby finger to each other. Rock the cradle.

Our House Is a Very Fine House

Here Is the Church

Here is the church,
*With hands back to back, intertwine
fingers and turn hands over.*
Here is the steeple,
*Raise and touch each index finger to the
other.*
Open the doors
Pull thumbs apart.
And see all the people.
*Turns hands back over showing all fingers
intertwined.*
Close the doors
Turn hands back over as in the beginning.
And hear them pray.
Hold hands near an ear.
Open the doors;
*Turn hands over showing intertwined
fingers.*
They all walk away.
*Separate hands and place them behind
your back.*

Here Is a House

Here is a house built up high,
*Reach arms over head with fingertips
touching.*
With two tall chimneys reaching the
sky.
Reach arms straight up over head.
Here are the windows,
*Touch fingertips and tips of thumbs togeth-
er to make a square shape.*
Here is the door.
Pantomime a knocking motion.
If we peep inside we'll see a mouse on
the floor.
*Raise hands over head and shake hands in
fright.*

The Wise Man

Verse 1

The wise man built his house up-on the rock, The wise man built his house up-on the rock, The wise man built his house up-on the rock, And the rain came tumb-ling down.

Verse 1 Chorus

The rain came down and the floods came up, The rain came down and the floods came up, The rain came down and the floods came up, And the house on the rock stood firm.

Motions for Verse 1

Pound fists together throughout the song.

Rain
Start with arms above head; wiggle fingers while moving arms down.

Motions for Verse 1 Chorus

Rain came down
Start with arms above head; wiggle fingers while moving arms down.

Floods came up
Lift hands, palms up, a little higher each time.

House on the rock stood firm.
Pound fists together once and hold them there.

Verse 2

The foolish man built his house
   upon the sand,
The foolish man built his house
   upon the sand,
The foolish man built his house
   upon the sand
And the rain came tumbling down.

Motions for Verse 2

Same motions as Verse 1

Verse 2 Chorus

The rain came down and the floods
   came up,
The rain came down and the floods
   came up,
The rain came down and the floods
   came up
And the house on the sand fell flat.

Motions for Verse 2 Chorus

Same motions as verse 1 Chorus until
House on the sand fell flat.
With palms down, move hands from crossed in front out to sides.

Carpenter's Hammer

The carpenter's hammer goes tap, tap, tap
Tap two fists together.
And his saw goes seesaw, see.
Make a push and pull motion with both hands.
He hammers and hammers
Tap fists together.
And saws and saws
Push, pull motion.
And he builds a house for me.
Reach hands above head, fingertips touching.

My Little House

My little house won't stand up straight,
Touch the fingertips of one hand to the fingertips of the other hand and rock hands side to side.
My little house has lost its gate.
Lower the two little fingers.
My little house bends up and down,
Rock hands with more motion.
My little house is the oldest in town.
Separate hands and continue to rock with more motion.
Here comes the wind; it blows and blows again,
Place hands together again and blow through thumbs.
Down falls my little house. Oh, what a shame!
Drop hands into lap.

The Roof of the House

This is the roof of the house so good,
Hold arms above head with fingertips touching.
These are the walls that are made out of wood.
Hold hands flat out in front.
These are the windows that let in the light,
Hold up thumb and index finger of each hand and touch thumbs together.
This is the door that shuts so tight.
With thumbs still touching, lift all fingers and close hands together.
This is the chimney straight and tall,
Fold hands and lift one finger.
What a good house for us, one and all.
Hold hands apart, palms up, and nod head twice.

Here Is the Chimney

Here is the chimney,
Hold up fist with thumb tucked inside.
Here is the top.
Place other hand on top of fist.
Open the lid
Remove top hand.
And out Santa will pop!
Pop up thumb from inside fist.

Winding Down

Wind, Wind, Wind the Bobbin

Wind, wind, wind the bob-bin, Wind, wind, wind the bob-bin.

Pull,   pull,   tap,   tap,   tap.

Verse & Motions

Wind, wind, wind the bobbin.
Wind, wind, wind the bobbin.
  Roll hands one over the other.
Pull, pull,
  Starting with hands close together, pull
  hands apart twice.
Tap, tap, tap.
  Tap fists together three times.

Help Me Wind My Ball of Wool

Help me wind my ball of wool,

Hold it gent - ly do not pull.

Wind the wool and wind the wool, a -

round, a - round, a - round.

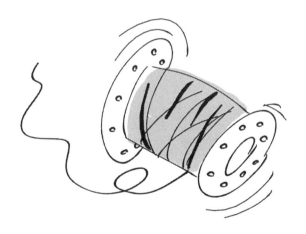

Motions

Wind one hand around the other hand.
Discover other body parts the wool can be
wound around. (head, ear, elbow, etc…)

Time for Bed

Ready for a Nap

This is the baby ready for a nap.
Hold up index finger.
Lay baby down in a loving lap.
Lay index finger in palm of other hand.
Cover baby up so s/he won't peep.
Close fingers of open hand around index finger.
Rock the baby till s/he's fast asleep.
Still holding finger, gently swing hands back and forth.

When I Am Sleepy

When I am sleepy and ready for bed,
Speak while yawning and rubbing eyes.
I kneel on the floor and bow my head.
After I pray, I turn out the lights,
Fold hands and then pretend to turn out lights by pulling on imaginary chain.
I pull up the covers all snug and tight.
Pretend to pull covers up to neck then cross arms hugging.

Sleepy Fingers

My fingers are so sleepy,
Close fingers one at a time as indicated throughout the rhyme.
It's time they went to bed.
So first, you Baby Finger,
Tuck in your little head.

Ringman, come, now it's your turn
And then comes Tallman great.
Now, Pointer Finger, hurry
Because it's getting late.

Let's see if all are snuggled.
No, here's one more to come.
So come, lie close, little brothers,
Make room for Master Thumb.
Fold thumb under other fingers.

ACTION SONGS

Animal Friends

My Big Gray Cat

My big gray cat is sound asleep,
  Sitting on the floor, rest head on hands.
All curled up in a little heap.
When he wakes up he'll stretch and
  purr
  Sit up and stretch.
Then wash his face and smooth his
  fur.
  Stroke face and stroke shoulders.
He'll stand up on his fine soft paws
  Place knees and hands on the floor.
And arch his back and show his claws.
  *Arch back and hold up hands with fingers
  bent.*
He'll scamper off to run and play.
  *Run fingers around on the floor and then
  behind your back.*
I love my gray cat more each day.
  Hug yourself and twist from side to side.

Hop Like a Bunny

We'll hop, hop, hop like a bunny
And run, run, run like a dog.
We'll walk, walk, walk like an elephant
And jump, jump, jump like a frog.
We'll swim, swim, swim like a goldfish
And fly, fly, fly like a bird.
We'll sit right down and fold our hands
And say not a single word.
  Perform motions as directed.

The Elephant

The elephant goes like this and that,
  *Alternately tap hands on thighs while
  standing.*
He's terribly big
  Reach arms up high.
And terribly fat.
  Spread arms out wide.
He has no fingers,
  Wiggle fingers.
He has no toes,
  Point to toes and wiggle toes.
But goodness, gracious, what a nose!
  *Clasp hands and lean over swinging arms
  from side to side.*

I Saw a Little Rabbit

I saw a little rabbit go hop, hop, hop.
  Hop three times.
I saw his ears go flop, flop, flop.
  *Flop hands over three times with thumbs
  touching temple.*
I saw his nose go wink, wink, wink.
  Wiggle nose three times.
I saw his eyes go blink, blink, blink.
  Blink three times.
I said, "Little rabbit, won't you stay?"
  Beckon with index finger.
He looked at me and hopped away.
  Hop.

My Little Puppy

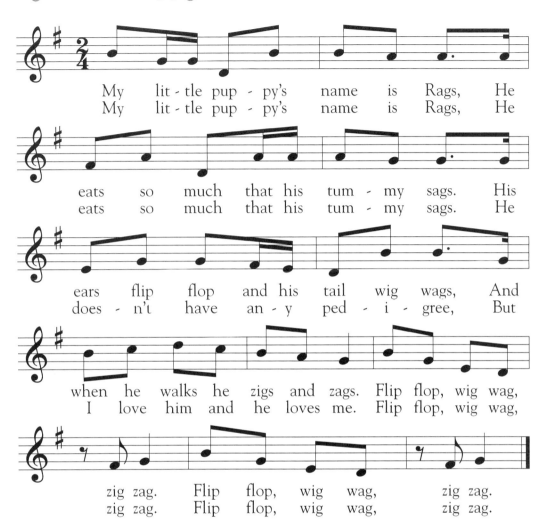

My lit-tle pup-py's name is Rags, He
My lit-tle pup-py's name is Rags, He

eats so much that his tum-my sags. His
eats so much that his tum-my sags. He

ears flip flop and his tail wig wags, And
does-n't have an-y ped-i-gree, But

when he walks he zigs and zags. Flip flop, wig wag,
I love him and he loves me. Flip flop, wig wag,

zig zag. Flip flop, wig wag, zig zag.
zig zag. Flip flop, wig wag, zig zag.

Motions

eats so much - *Rub tummy.*
tummy sags - *Arms curved under tummy.*
flip flop - *Tap head with each hand.*
wig wags - *Hips sway side to side.*
zigs and zags - *Snap fingers.*
I love him - *Hand on heart, other hand out.*
and he - *Both hands out.*
loves me - *Both hands on heart.*

Alice the Camel

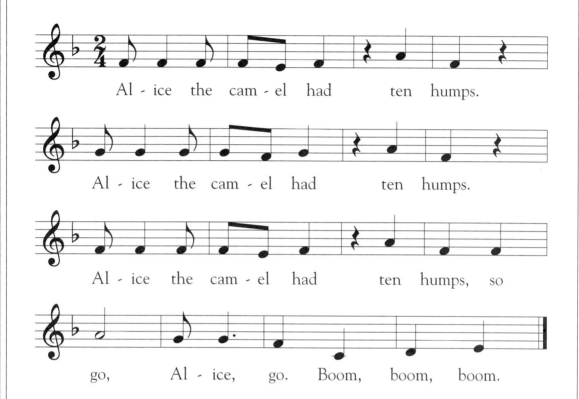

Al - ice the cam - el had ten humps.

Al - ice the cam - el had ten humps.

Al - ice the cam - el had ten humps, so

go, Al - ice, go. Boom, boom, boom.

Motions

Stand in a fairly tight circle. Show ten fingers for the first three lines.

go
  Put one hand into the center of the circle.

Alice
  Remove the first hand and put the other hand into the center of the circle.

go
  Remove the second hand and put the first hand back into the center of the circle.

boom
  *On each "boom," bump hips with neighbors; to one side, to the other side and then
  back to the original.*

  *Repeat the song with one less finger and sing "nine humps." Continue singing verses
  until "no humps."*

Mother Goonie Bird

Moth-er Goon-ie Bird had sev-en chicks, sev-en

chicks had Moth - er Goon - ie Bird, And they

could - n't walk, And they could-n't talk, But they

all could go like this. "Right wing"

Additional Verses

Once started, do not stop motions until the end of the song.

Verse 1
At the end of verse one begin flapping right arm with the beat.

Verse 2
Left wing
Flap both arms with the beat.

Verse 3
Right foot
Continue flapping arms and lift right knee up and down.

Verse 4
Left foot
Flap both arms and alternately lift knees.

Verse 5
Now your head
In addition to all previous motions push chin out and in.

Verse 6
Sit down
At the end of this verse stop all motions and sit down.

Head & Shoulders, Knees & Toes

Toes, Knees, Chest, Nut

Toes, knees, chest, nut,
> *While standing place both hands on toes, on
> knees, on chest and on head.*

Touch your fingers to the ground.
> *Touch ground.*

Toes, knees, chest, nut,
> *While standing place both hands on toes, on
> knees, on chest and on head.*

Everybody turn around.
> *All turn around.*

Toes, knees, chest, nut,
> *While standing place both hands on toes, on
> knees, on chest and on head.*

Touch your fingers to the ground.
> *Touch ground.*

Toes, knees, chest, nut,
> *While standing place both hands on toes, on
> knees, on chest and on head.*

All sit down.
> *Sit down.*

Oliver Twist

O - li - ver Twist, you can't do this so

what's the use of try - ing?

Touch your knees, touch your toes,

Clap your hands and a - round you go.

Motons

Stand and perform motions as indicated.

Head and Shoulders Baby

Head and shoul - ders ba - by one,

two, three. Head and shoul - ders ba - by

one, two, three. Head and

shoul - ders, head and shoul - ders, head and shoul - ders ba - by

one, two, three.

Motions

head
Touch head.
shoulders
Touch shoulders.
baby
Clap hands.
one
Tap legs then clap.
two
Tap legs then clap.
three
Tap legs.

Verse 2

Knees and ankles, baby...
Tap body parts as mentioned and clap as in Verse 1.

Improvise and perform motions for other verses such as:
Comb your hair, baby...
Milk the cow, baby...

Head and Shoulders

Head   and   shoul - ders,   knees   and   toes,   knees   and   toes.

Head   and   shoul - ders,   knees   and   toes,   knees   and   toes.   My

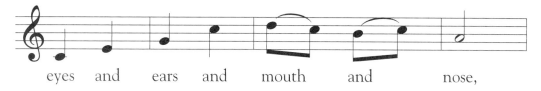

eyes   and   ears   and   mouth   and   nose,

Head   and   shoul - ders,   knees   and   toes,   knees   and   toes.

Motions

*Stand and touch each body part as it is
mentioned in the song. Repeat the song
several times, each time singing faster and
faster.*

Hang About

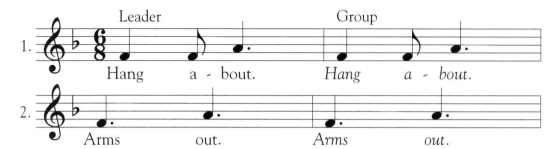

Hang a - bout. Hang a - bout.

Arms out. Arms out.

All chant: Dum de da, dum de da, dum de da da da Swing arms back and forth

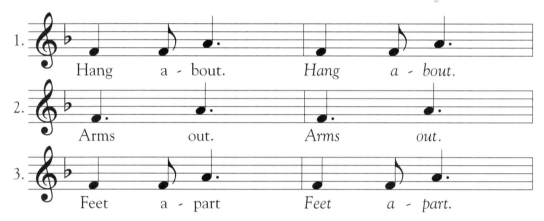

Hang a - bout. Hang a - bout.

Arms out. Arms out.

Feet a - part Feet a - part.

All chant: Dum de da, dum de da, dum de da da da Swing arms back and forth

Knees to - geth - er. Knees to - geth - er.

Do 1, 2, 3 then 4 followed by the chant: Dum de da, dum de da, dum de da da da

Bot - tom's out. Bot - tom's out.

Do 1, 2, 3, 4 then 5 followed by the chant: Dum de da, dum de da, dum de da da da

Tongue's out. Tongue's out.

Do 1, 2, 3, 4, 5 then 6 followed by the chant with tongue still out:
Dum de da, dum de da, dum de da da da

The Jack-in-the-Box

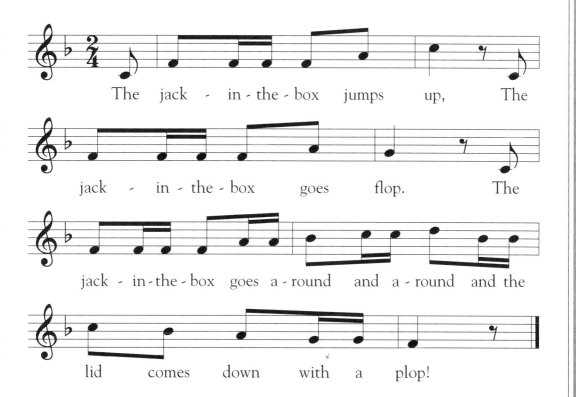

The jack - in - the - box jumps up, The jack - in - the - box goes flop. The jack - in - the - box goes a - round and a - round and the lid comes down with a plop!

Motions

The jack-in-the-box jumps up,
   Jump up from a crouched position.
The jack-in-the-box goes flop,
   Bend over from the waist with arms hanging down.

The jack-in-the-box goes around and around
   While bent over, turn around once in place.
And the lid comes down with a flop.
   Slowly lower to the ground, ready to begin again.

Pick a Bale of Cotton

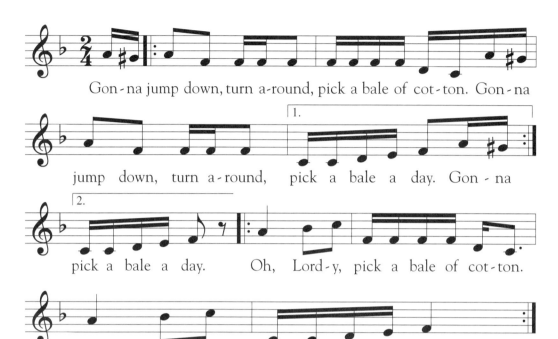

Gon-na jump down, turn a-round, pick a bale of cot-ton. Gon-na

jump down, turn a-round, pick a bale a day. Gon-na

pick a bale a day. Oh, Lord-y, pick a bale of cot-ton.

Oh, Lord-y, pick a bale a day.

Motions

Perform the following motions each times those words occur.

jump down
  Touch the floor.
turn around
  Turn around once.
pick a bale
  Tap both hands onto thighs.
oh, Lordy
  Move hands in an upward flutter.

Hop Up and Jump Up

Part 1: *Jump 4 times and turn around once. Reach arms out and turn around twice more.*

Part 2: *Repeat Part 1.*

Part 3: *Reach arms out and turn around twice. Reach up and reach down. Turn around once.*

Part 4: *Repeat Part 3.*

Going Places, Doing Things

In the Apple Tree

Away up high in the apple tree,
Stand holding hands above head.
Two little apples smiled at me.
Point to yourself and smile.
I shook that tree as hard as I could,
Pretend to shake the tree with both hands.
Down came the apples,
Bring fists down to the ground.
Ummmm, they were good!
Rub tummy.

Marco Polo

Marco Polo went to France.
Tap on head.
Taught the ladies how to dance.
Swing hips from side to side with hands on hips.
First a kick, then a bow,
Kick foot up, then bow.
Marco Polo showed them how.
Tap on legs.

The Wind Came Out to Play

The wind came out to play one day,
Begin in crouched position and quickly stand up.
He swept the clouds out of his way.
Sway back and forth with arms stretched up.
He blew the leaves and away they flew.
Flutter hands down.
The trees bent low, and their branches too.
Bend over with arms hanging down.
The wind blew the great big ships at the sea.
Sweep hanging arms back and forth.
The wind blew my kite away from me.
Stand up and shade eyes with one hand while pointing to the sky with the other hand.

There Once Was a Man

There once was a man who was tall, tall, tall.
Stand up.
He had a friend who was small, small, small.
Sit down.
The man who was small would call to the man that was tall,
Still sitting, look up with hand to mouth.
"Hello up there."
And the man
Stand up.

Who was tall would call to the man that was small,
Still standing, look down with hand to mouth.
"Hello down there."
Then they each tipped their hat,
Pretend to tip hat.
And made this reply,
"Good-bye, my friend."
Wave to the floor and sit down.
"Good-bye."
Still sitting, look up and wave.

I'm a Little Teapot

I'm a lit - tle tea - pot short and stout,

Here is my han - dle, Here is my spout.

When I get all steamed up hear me shout, Just

tip me o - ver and pour me out.

Verse 1

I'm a little teapot short and stout,
  Stand still.
Here is my handle,
  Place one hand on hip.
Here is my spout.
  Make an "s" shape with other arm.
When I get all steamed up hear me
  shout,
Just tip me over and pour me out.
  *Lean over on the side with the "s" shaped
  arm.*

Verse 2

I can change my handle and my
  spout,
Now here is my handle and here is
  my spout.
  Switch positions of both arms.
When I get all steamed up hear me
  shout,
Just tip me over and pour me out.
  *Lean over on the side with the "s"
  shaped arm.*

Cousin Peter

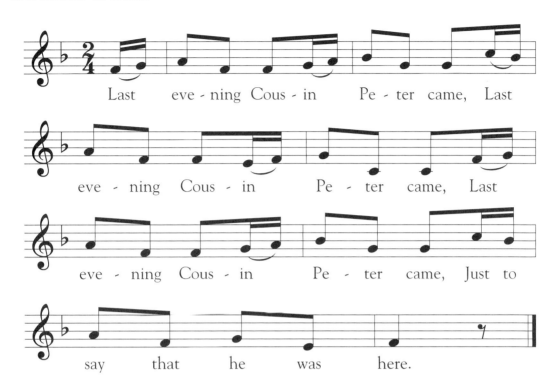

Last eve - ning Cous - in Pe - ter came, Last

eve - ning Cous - in Pe - ter came, Last

eve - ning Cous - in Pe - ter came, Just to

say that he was here.

Verse 1

Last evening cousin Peter came...

Walk in place.

Verse 2

He wiped his feet upon the mat...

Alternately wipe feet.

Verse 3

He hung his hat upon the peg...

Alternately touch head and reach hand out in front.

Verse 4

He played he was a great big bear...

With both arms up rock back and forth.

Verse 5

He picked me up into the air...

Alternately reach low and lift both hands up into the air.

Verse 6

He made a bow and said, "Good-bye."

Alternately bow and wave "good-bye."

When I Was One

When I was one I ate a bun, Go - ing o - ver the

sea. I jumped a - board a pi - rate ship and the

pi - rate said to me: "Go - ing o - ver, go - ing un - der, Stand at at-

ten - tion, like a sol - dier, With a one, two, three!"

Verse 1 & Motions

Hold up the correct number of fingers for each verse.

When I was one I ate a bun,
Hold up one finger.

Going over the sea.
Make waves with your hand.

I jumped aboard a pirate ship
Jump forward one step.

And the pirate said to me:
Point to someone else for "pirate" and to yourself for "me."

"Going over,
Reach hands out in front.

Going under,
Pull hands back and down completing the circular motions.

Stand at attention, like a soldier,
Salute.

With a one, two, three!"
Stomp feet three times.

Additional Verses

2 ...two, I buckled my shoe...
3 ...three, I climbed a tree...
4 ...four, I shut the door...
5 ...five, I took a dive...
6 ...six, I got in a fix...
7 ...seven, I went to heaven...
8 ...eight, I climbed a gate...
9 ...nine, I tickled my spine...
10 ...ten, I started again...

The Noble Duke of York

Oh, the No-ble Duke of York, He had ten thou-sand

men, He marched them up to the top of the hill and he

marched them down a - gain. Oh, and when you're up, you're

up, And when you're down, you're down, And when you're on-ly

half - way up, You're half - way to the ground.

Motions
Start in a stooping position.

ten thousand men
Spread arms wide apart.
up the hill
Stand up.
down the hill
Stoop down.
when you're up
Stand up.
when you're down
Stoop down.
half way
Stoop down half way and balance with arms extended apart.

Wake Up You Lazy Bones

Wake up you la-zy bones and go and fetch the cat - tle.

Fine

Wake up you la-zy bones and go and fetch the cows.

The cows are gone, the sun is hot,

D.C. al Fine

I think I'll rest, 'Til they come home.

Verse & Motions

Jump up and down during the first two phrases.

The cows are gone
   Place one knee on the floor.
The sun is hot
   Place both knees on the floor.
I think I'll rest
   Also place one elbow on the floor.
'Till they come home
   *With both elbows on the floor rest head on
   hands and close eyes.*

*Wait for different lengths of time then slap the
floor and shout "Wake up you lazy bones!"
Jump up as the song repeats from the beginning.*

A Sailor Went to Sea

A sail - or went to sea, sea, sea, to see what he could see, see, see, And all that he could see, see, see, was the bot - tom of the deep blue sea, sea, sea.

Verse 1

Salute each time you sing the word "sea" or "see."

Verse 2

A sailor went to chop, chop, chop...
Each time you sing the word "chop" make a chopping motion with one hand onto the other arm.

Verse 3

A sailor went to knee, knee, knee...
Each time you sing the word "knee" tap on your knees.

Verse 4

A sailor went to tap, tap, tap...
Each time you sing the word "tap" tap your foot on the ground.

Verse 5

A sailor went to oo-wachee wa...
Each time you sing "oo-wachee wa" wiggle your hips.

Verse 6

A sailor went to sea, chop, knee, tap, oo-wachee wa...
Do all five motions in order each time they occur in the song.

Index